HARNESS RACING

BY
ELIZABETH VAN STEENWYK

EDITED BY
DR. HOWARD SCHROEDER
Professor In Reading and Language Arts
Dept. of Elementary Education
Mankato State University

DESIGNED & PRODUCED BY
BAKER STREET PRODUCTIONS
MANKATO, MINNESOTA

COVER GRAPHICS BY
BOB WILLIAMS

CRESTWOOD HOUSE
Mankato, Minnesota

LIBRARY OF CONGRESS CATALOGING IN PUBLICATION DATA
Van Steenwyk, Elizabeth.
 Harness racing.

 (Horses, pasture to paddock)
 SUMMARY: Discusses the buying, breeding, and training of horses for harness racing, describes the event and its rules, and introduces several famous champions.
 1. Harness racing–Juvenile literature. (1. Harness racing. 2. Horse racing.) I. Schroeder, Howard. II. Baker Street Productions. III. Title. IV. Series.
 SF339.V36   1983   798.4'6   83-7598
 ISBN 0-89686-226-7

>   International Standard   Library of Congress
>   Book Numbers: Catalog Card Number:
>   Library Binding 0-89686-226-7   83-7598

PHOTOGRAPH CREDITS
Alix Coleman: Cover, 4, 6, 7, 17, 25
Hall of Fame of the Trotter: 9, 10, 15, 18, 45
Minnesota Historical Society: 13, 14
Joseph Berke: 20, 22, 32, 33, 37, 40-41
U.S. Trotting Association: 21, 23, 26, 27, 31, 43
Mary Phelps Photography: 28
United Press International: 34-35
Kentucky Horse Park, Lexington, KY: 38

CRESTWOOD HOUSE
Hwy. 66 South, Box 3427
Mankato, MN 56002-3427

Copyright© 1983 by Crestwood House, Inc. All rights reserved. No part of this book may be reproduced in any form without written permission from the publisher, except for brief passages included in a review. Printed in the United States of America.

TABLE OF CONTENTS

Introduction 5
1. Harness Racing History 8
    Pacers & Trotters
    Two Famous Horses
    The Automobile Appears
    The Sport Grows
2. The Horse and Its Equipment ... 17
    The Sulky
    The Tack
3. Buying, Breeding and Training .. 23
    Breeding a Standardbred
    Training the Harness Horse
    "Talking" to the Horse
4. Racing 31
    The Race
    Types of Races
5. The Cast of Characters 38
    Owners and Breeders
    Trainers and Drivers
    Special Help
6. After Racing Days Are Over.... 44
Glossary 46

Thanks to Mr. Dick Fineberg and the Golden Bear Raceway in Sacramento, California.

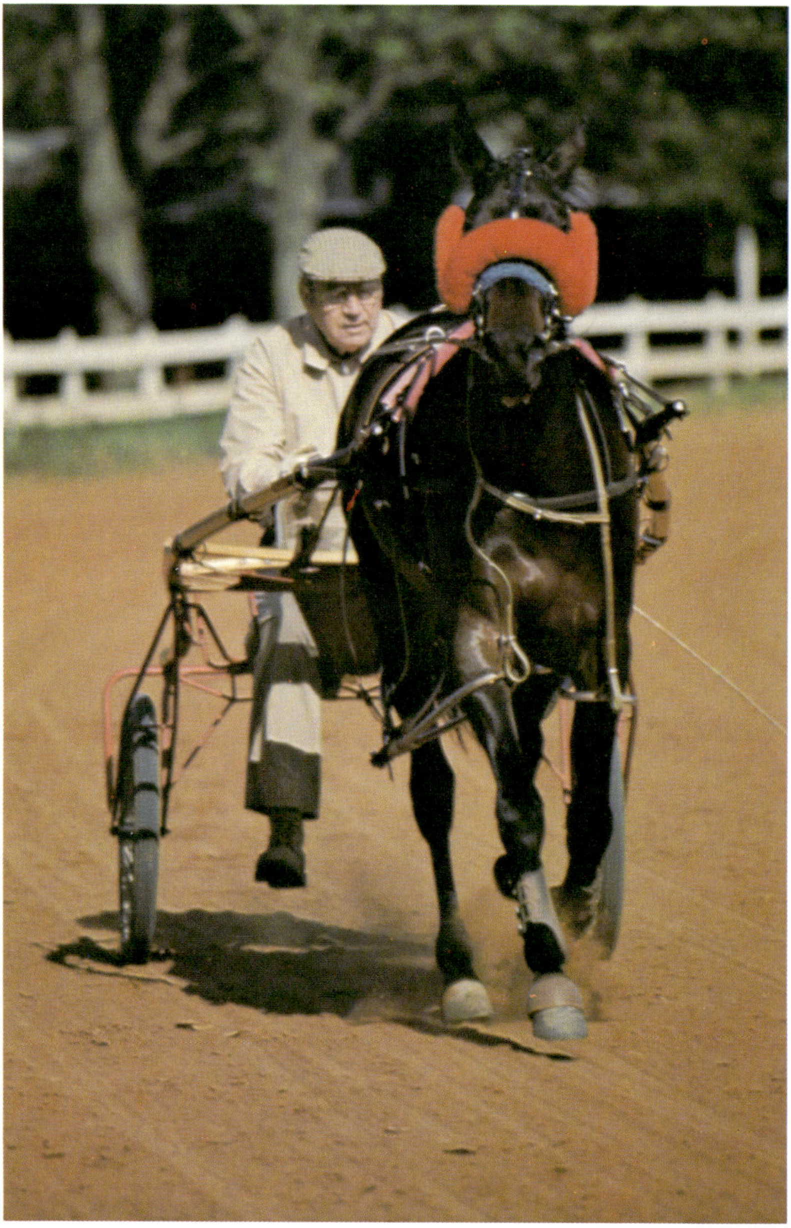

INTRODUCTION

It's a beautiful day for a horse race. The sun is shining and flowers bloom at the edge of thick, green lawns near the grandstand. The race track is crowded with excited people. Some of them are sitting in the grandstand. Others are standing near the outside rail at the edge of the track. All of them are watching the horses lining up by the starting gate.

But this is not just any horse race. This is harness racing and these horses are pulling small two-wheeled carts called sulkies. Drivers are sitting in these carts behind the horses.

The horses are beautiful and strong. Their coats shine as they paw the ground. A black horse named Dancer is one of the favorites. So is a brown horse, named Blaze. Which one will win today? No one knows for sure.

The horses line up behind the starting gate. The gate is attached to a vehicle. As the vehicle picks up speed, the horses move with it. The gate swings out of the way and the race is on! Dancer runs behind one of the other horses on the outside rail. He is covered up, which means the horse ahead is breaking the wind and may tire more quickly. Coming out of the first turn, Blaze goes ahead before he can be boxed in by other horses. Now Dancer moves ahead at the second turn. In front of the grandstand, a third horse makes a move to take the lead. Blaze is losing ground.

The horses begin their second trip around the track since they are running a mile on a half-mile track. Dancer is running well, but where's Blaze? Has he lost so much ground that he won't be able to catch up? No. He's battling with another horse on the backstretch, showing he has a good burst of speed. The horses' manes and tails are flying in the wind.

Now Blaze moves up close to Dancer as they round the final turn. It's going to be a battle down to the finish wire. The drivers lightly touch the horses with their whips. The whip doesn't hurt them. It only reminds the horses to run faster.

The starting gate has pulled away and the race is on!

The crowd in the grandstand and near the fence is shouting and cheering. The horses feel excited too, and want to win the race as much as the people want them to win. It's going to be close. The horses are neck-and-neck down the homestretch. Who will the winner be, Dancer or Blaze? Down toward the finish line they run, closer, ever closer. And then, just at the end, Blaze crosses the finish line first.

A cheer goes up from the crowd. Blaze walks slowly to the winner's circle to receive the traditional blanket of flowers from a racing official. Blaze's owner receives a trophy. Then Blaze returns to his stall in the paddock area for a drink of water and

The race to the finish.

some rest before the next race. It's been a beautiful day for a race. It's even more beautiful when you win.

1
HARNESS RACING HISTORY

The sport of harness racing dates back in history many years. Some history books tell us it is thousands of years old. We know that there were harness races in the Olympics as early as 1,000 B.C. Wherever there were horses pulling carts or wagons, there were probably races of some kind.

In England during the 1700's, mail and stage coaches were often matched in contests on back country roads. In the United States at that time, there were hardly any races because there were few roads before 1800.

However, 1788, is an important date in American harness racing. In that year a great horse, named Messenger, was brought to the United States from England. He is thought to be the founding sire, or father, of all champion trotting horses in the United States. Messenger lived on breeding farms in the eastern part of the country and sired many future champions.

Hambletonian is thought to be the next most

important horse in U.S. harness racing history. He is a great-grandson of Messenger. This gentle bay horse was bought by a man named William Rysdyk. Mr. Rysdyk paid $125 for Hambletonian shortly after he was foaled in 1849. That was quite a bit of money in 1849. Mr. Rysdyk had to borrow most of that money to pay for the horse. However, before the horse died in 1876, he had earned Mr. Rysdyk a great deal of money because he sired so many Stand-

Messenger.

ardbreds (the official name for harness racing horses). Today, every horse racing in harness is one of Hambletonian's relatives. The most important race for three-year-old trotters, the Hambletonian is named after him.

PACERS & TROTTERS

There are two types of horses used for harness racing — pacers and trotters. Pacers came from a

Hambletonian.

part of the country called Narragansett Bay in Rhode Island. Originally, they were known as saddle horses, because their gait made them comfortable to ride. George Washington liked the Narragansett Bay horses and used them on important trips. Paul Revere rode one on his famous ride in 1775. Over the years the two types of horses were developed by people interested in harness racing.

What's a trotter? The answer is in its gait, or the way in which a horse moves its legs. A trotter moves its right front and left rear legs forward at the same time. Then its left front and right rear legs come forward together.

A pacer has a different gait. Its right legs, both front and rear, move forward together. Then its left legs, both front and rear, move forward together.

No one knows exactly when trotters and pacers first began racing in the United States. Most people agree that it was in the late 1700's. However, the horses were still being ridden with saddles in those early races, which were held in open fields. They were not hitched to any wheeled carts or buggies.

As America's roads began to improve, some early racing buggies appeared. They looked much like regular four-wheel buggies or wagons in use at that time. Everyone laughed when these buggies were first driven in races. But the new buggies soon became very popular because they were fun to drive. The sport of harness racing was born.

Around 1840, a two-wheeled buggy began to be used. The new buggy or "bike," had high wheels and the driver could see over the horse. Horses were soon breaking speed records pulling these new two-wheeled bikes.

Racing under saddle all but disappeared in the 1870's as the new buggies gained in popularity.

The sport of harness racing grew as the United States grew. Farmers enjoyed the sport and took it with them as they moved west. They had always loved the pacers and raced them in midwest county fairs whenever they had a chance. If it hadn't been for these people, the racing world may have lost an important part of harness racing.

TWO FAMOUS HORSES

Goldsmith Maid was a granddaughter of the great Hambletonian. Foaled in 1855, she didn't race until she was eight years old. She started late in life for a Standardbred and raced until she was twenty. Goldsmith Maid won 119 races. She was strong and fast, and attracted huge crowds everywhere she went. People loved her because she tried hard to win every race she entered.

No horse in harness racing history is as well known as Dan Patch. He became famous in story and song because he was a real champion. Dan Patch was foaled in 1896, and began to race when he was four years old. M.W. Savage bought him for $60,000 in 1902. The next year Dan Patch set a record for a one-mile race with a time of 1:56¼. The following year he broke his own record with a time of 1:56.

Dan Patch soon became so famous that items were named for him. Children rode on Dan Patch wagons and sleds. Men smoked Dan Patch cigars and women used Dan Patch washing machines. Songs and stories were written about him. Dan

Dan Patch racing to another victory at the Minnesota State Fair in 1906.

Dan Patch and Mr. M.W. Savage.

Patch traveled from race to race in his own railroad car. Wherever he raced, people lined the streets from the railroad depot to the track so they could touch him.

After racing for ten years and never losing, Dan Patch retired. He died on July 11, 1916. His owner, Mr. Savage, died the following day.

THE AUTOMOBILE APPEARS

People continued to enjoy harness racing through the early 1900's. At that time, they still depended on the horse and buggy to take them where they wanted to go. When the automobile came along, the horse was no longer "king" of the road. For a while, people only wanted to race cars, not horses. Many race tracks went out of business in the 1920's and 1930's.

In 1935, when there was little excitement in harness racing, a horse named Greyhound began setting speed records. He was called the grey ghost because of his color as well as his speed. The grey ghost didn't win a lot of money, because there wasn't much to win in those days. But many people say that his exciting speed saved harness racing.

In 1940, the United States Trotting Association was formed. This Association brought organization

Greyhound.

and rules to the sport for trotters and pacers. It was not until after World War II, however, that the sport really began to grow again. One reason was due to an automobile-mounted starting gate.

Before the new gate was used, it could sometimes take the starter of a race almost an hour to line up the horses. Spectators grew impatient and fewer races could be run. With the new starting gate, the horses got off to an even start easily and quickly.

New race tracks were built as the sport grew. Lights were added for nighttime harness racing. The amounts of winning prize money grew larger and larger. The breeding of horses became better and more scientific. Once again, harness racing was popular.

THE SPORT GROWS

One of the best horses during this time was Adios. Adios set six world records during his racing days in the 1940's. Once he ran two of his best races, one after the other, on the same day. A new owner bought him in 1955, for a record $500,000.

Adios is believed to be one of the greatest pacing sires of all time. For nine straight years his sons and daughters led the list in money won for their owners. In addition, fifty-seven of his sons and daughters ran a one-mile race in two minutes or less.

Adios died in 1965, but he left behind many offspring. These offspring continue to win and break records even today.

In the 1980's harness racing is better known than ever before. Nearly thirty million people attend the races each year in the United States. They go to one of the sixty tracks around the country or one of the four hundred summertime fairs. Harness racing enjoys equal popularity with fans in Canada and many countries in Europe. Among the leading raceways in Canada are the Greenwood Raceway in Toronto, Connaught Park in Lucerne, and Richelieu Park in Montreal.

② THE HORSE AND ITS EQUIPMENT

A Standardbred is an American breed, or family,

of horse used for harness racing. During this country's early years, thoroughbred horses were bred to light-harness horses. Their foals, or offspring, were stronger and heavier than their thoroughbred parent. They were also shorter and more gentle, but just as brave. They liked to work hard. Soon these horses became known as a true breed. The name, Standardbred, was given to this new breed by the National Association of Trotting Horse Breeders.

THE SULKY

Today's sulky, a modern name for the buggy, is a light two-wheel carriage. It wasn't always that way. The early sulkies, or "bikes," as they were called, were heavy and had wooden wheels with broad tires. The wheels were very tall and the driver sat high

Pictured above is an example of an early sulky.

18

above the horse. For nearly one hundred years, drivers on these high wheeled sulkies raced toward a goal they would never reach - the two-minute mile. Then the bicycle wheel came along in 1892, and changed it all.

A lot of people had tried to make sulkies using smaller wheels. Nothing really worked well until a man named Sterling Elliot came up with a new idea. He was the owner of a bicycle factory. One day, Mr. Elliot took the wheels off a bicycle and put them on a sulky. A driver hitched the sulky to a horse named Excellence. He won the first race he entered. A few weeks later, a trotter named Nancy Hanks raced to a new world's record using the new bicycle wheels.

Builders of sulkies made more changes over the next few years. Sometimes the changes improved the sulky; sometimes they didn't. But soon the sulky became lighter, stronger, and safer.

Many of today's sulkies are still made of hardwood, although aluminum and steel are also used. If you ordered a sulky from the factory, you would get one that was about fifty inches wide and twenty-seven inches high. The wheels would be twenty-eight inches in diameter. The sulky would weigh about forty pounds.

Often a sulky will be built especially for one certain horse. Different-sized horses need different-sized sulkies to pull, just as they need different-sized harnesses to wear. Once the sulky size for a certain

Sulkies today are built lighter, stronger, and safer.

horse is decided upon, a card will go from race track to race track bearing the size for that horse. Then the horse will always have the right size sulky to race in. Some owners ship their own custom-built sulky to the race track.

THE TACK

The equipment any horse wears is called the tack. A horse will have a tack box, or trunk, in the stable for this equipment. Most trained horses wear tack such as bridles, girth, bit, and blanket. Harness horses, however, wear much more.

Pacers wear hobbles, or leather straps. These hobbles connect the front and rear legs on the same side so they will move forward and backward together. Both pacers and trotters wear a checkrein to hold

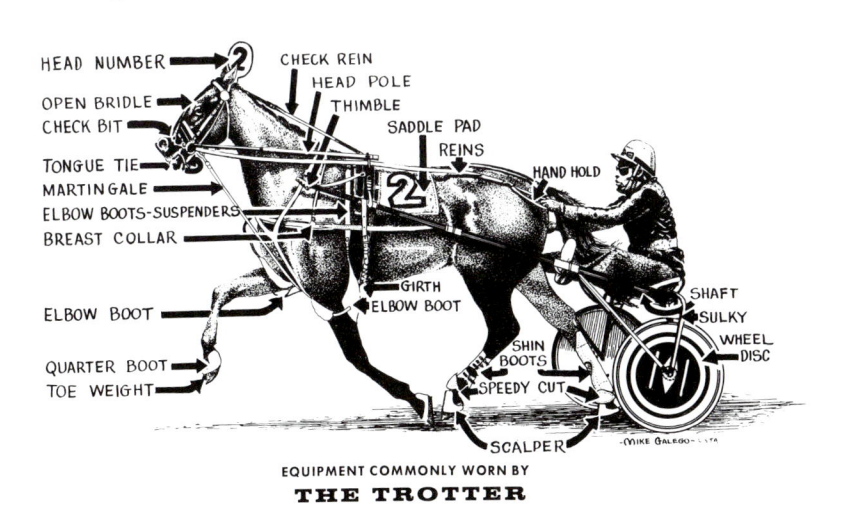

EQUIPMENT COMMONLY WORN BY
THE TROTTER

A close-up of harness tack on a trotter's head.

their heads high, so they will keep the right stride and balance. Both pacers and trotters also wear boots, which are pads for their knees, shins, ankles, and elbows. These pads keep the horses from hurting themselves as they run. Trotters as well as pacers wear a number on head poles above their heads while racing. Head poles tell people in the grandstand who the horse is by the number printed on the pole. Although the horses don't wear saddles, they do wear saddle pads. The same number as the one on their head poles is on the saddle pad.

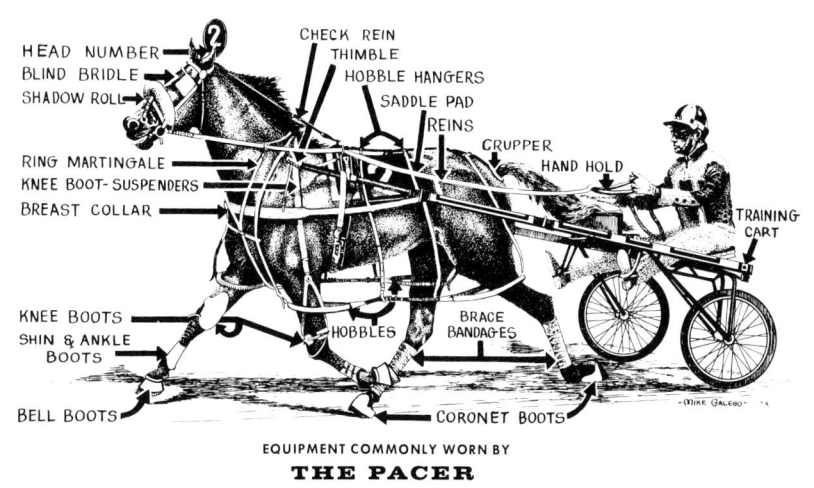

EQUIPMENT COMMONLY WORN BY
THE PACER

③ BUYING, BREEDING AND TRAINING

People who buy harness horses must be careful to

23

check several things before spending any money. First they study the "papers" on a horse, which are records of the sire and the dam (father and mother) and its brothers and sisters.

Next they study the horse. How much was it sold for before this sale? Has it won any races? Has it missed any races it should have been in? Why?

Finally, the buyer wants to see the horse. If possible the buyer will watch the horse race. If a trainer or veterinarian is available, the buyer will ask them to look at the horse, too. The expert can also help the would be owner look for good qualities, such as a wide chest, straight legs and well-shaped hoofs.

There are many places to buy a Standardbred. Some people like to go to claiming races at nearby tracks. A claiming race is one where any horse in the field may be bought for the price given that day by its owner. A claiming slip and a check must be given to the track officials before the race begins. After the race, the new owner "claims" the horse. A claimed horse can be racing for its new owner in about a week's time.

Other people like to attend horse auctions. An auction is a sale at which goods are sold to the person offering the most money. Many yearlings, or year old horses, are sold at auctions.

Picking a winner in a young horse takes a lot of skill and experience. It also takes a lot of patience, since a young horse will not be racing for at least one year. The new owner has to wait to see if the choice made was a good one.

Horses may also be bought at private sales, that is, from other owners. Another way to get a harness horse is by breeding and raising the foal from birth.

BREEDING A STANDARDBRED

Some people like to buy a mare, or female horse, and breed her to a stallion, or male horse. Then they raise the foal. Of course, this takes much longer than buying a fully grown horse. It takes about three and a half years from the time of breeding to the animal's first race.

The choice of mare and stallion is very important.

An early morning workout at the track.

The way they look and act will often decide how good the foal will be. The foal may look and act like either parent.

About 340 days after breeding, the mare will foal, or give birth. A foal grows to about eighty percent of its full size in the first twelve months of life.

TRAINING THE HARNESS HORSE

Training starts when the horse is a yearling. (All harness horses have an official birthday on January 1, no matter what date in the year they are born.) The horse is fitted with shoes before any training begins. Just as no two children have the exact same foot size, no two yearlings have the same hoof size. Some

A farrier puts on a new horseshoe.

yearlings will need a twelve ounce shoe, while others can wear shoes half that weight.

Yearlings must first be taught to lead, that is, to follow when a rope is attached to its halter. While this is being done, the young horse is also getting to know the trainer's voice and hands.

Harnessing is next. The horse is allowed to smell the harness first, then it is gently laid on the animal's back. Slowly, the rest of the harness tack is put on the yearling, including the bit, or metal bar that fits into its mouth. Then the trainer will let the yearling walk around by itself. When the horse begins to feel comfortable with the tack it is ready to be walked around the stable yard by the trainer. Finally, long lines, or reins, are put on the harness and the horse is line driven, or walked with the trainer behind while holding the lines. As soon as the yearling has learned

A trainer line drives this young harness horse.

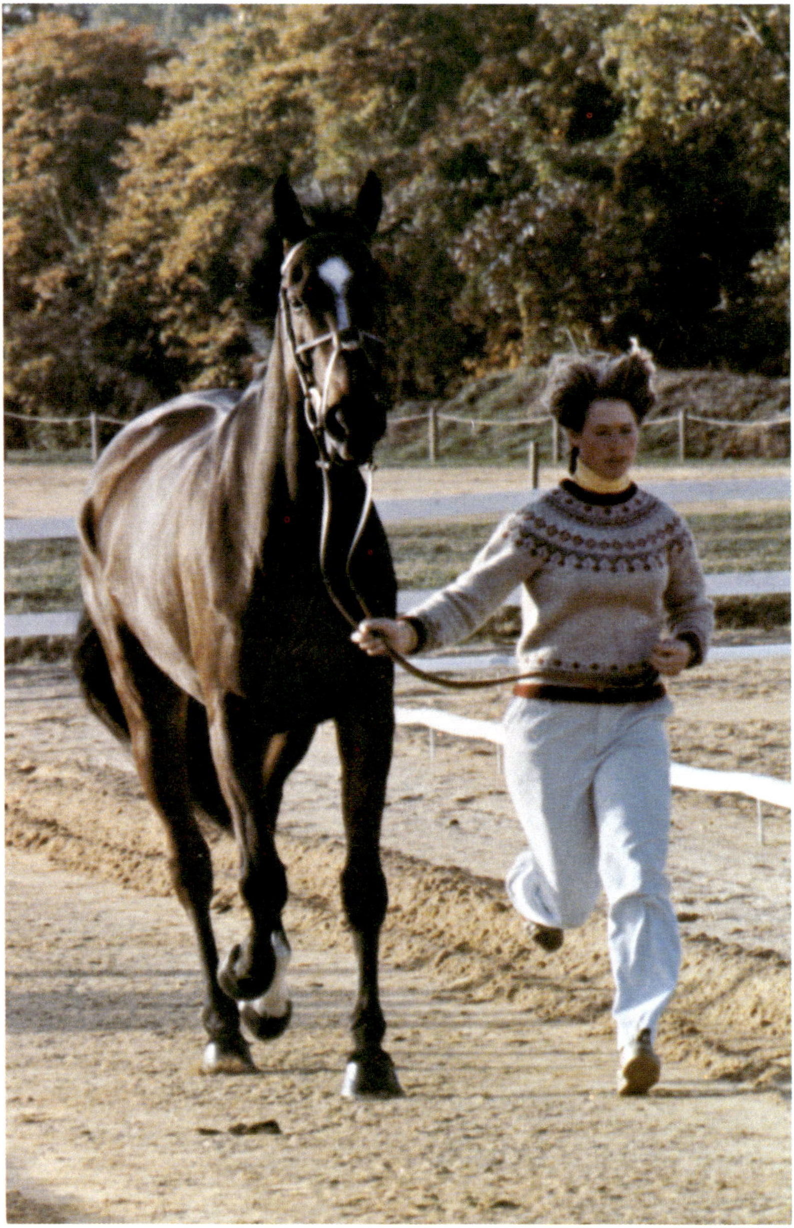

this lesson, it is ready to be hitched to a jog, or training, cart.

The first few times a horse is hitched to a cart it may be scared. As the horse becomes used to the cart, it will learn to walk past other horses, carts, and people without being upset. During this time the yearling will also start jogging while pulling a cart.

"TALKING" TO THE HORSE

The horse and trainer need to know and understand one another very well. The tools used to do this are the voice, hands, lines, and a whip.

A horse needs to understand several words or sounds quickly. By understanding the word "whoa," a horse will learn to stop, slow down, or relax, depending upon the trainer's tone of voice. "Clucking" to a horse is also very important and can be taught early. Once a horse learns it should hurry up, it will not have to be slapped with a line or tapped with a whip to get it to move faster. Other words such as "come here," are also taught to a horse to get its attention.

Sometimes a horse must be "spanked" with the lines. This does not hurt the horse, but gets its attention when the trainer needs to steer it away from something in its path. Teaching a horse to go around a turn on the track is another time when it may need to be spanked by the harness lines. Many horses slow down in a turn and move closer to the fence. A quick spank on the horse's inside hip will drive it away from the fence and it will take the turn properly.

Many trainers do not use a whip on a young horse because they believe it makes the horse nervous and harder to train. When the whip is used, it is only to tell the horse what your hands and voice tell it. The whip is never used to punish a horse.

The young horse's jogging distance is slowly increased to about four miles a day. The horse's muscles get stronger and so does its breathing. Slowly the horse's race against the clock gets better. By the time it is two years old and ready for its first race, the horse can run at least a three-minute mile.

The horse is also learning good manners during this time. It is learning to behave in the stall, to pass and be passed on the track, to walk to and from the track, and to walk quietly when cooling out after a jog.

Horses in training get good daily care. They have clean, well-bedded stalls for proper rest, and the best food for strength. Horses are kept clean, wear clean equipment and are rubbed down after training. "You can't expect a horse to give you more than you are willing to give it," is the way a top trainer puts it.

④ RACING

Harness horses race at their best around the ages of four, five and six. Some may race until they are fifteen years old — the oldest year in which they are allowed to race. A harness horse's training goes on during its entire racing life though. Before a race is run, the horse may run five, six, or more miles in a warm-up pulling a jog cart. Trotters and pacers need

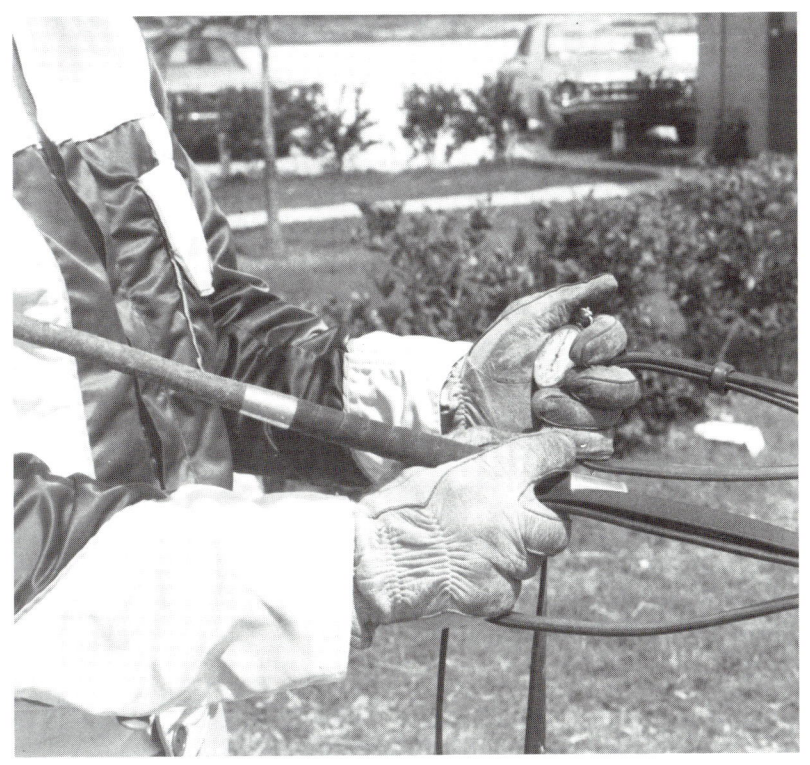

The driver checks a horse's time after a workout.

this run to loosen their muscles, in the same way that long distance runners need to warm-up. Before lining up for a race, the horse is harnessed to its sulky and run down the homestretch several times. Then the horses are brought to the starting gate which is fastened on a car or truck. After the horses are lined up, the starting gate begins to move. It slowly speeds up to thirty-five miles an hour, which is the speed of the start. When the sides of the gate fold forward against the vehicle, the race is on.

THE RACE

In harness races, pacers race only pacers and trotters race only trotters. Once the race is under way,

Prior to a race, the horses are in the paddock area.

the driver's understanding of a horse's speed and gait takes over. The driver will know when and how to guide a horse in the race. Sometimes a driver will guide the horse to the inside rail behind the lead horses. As the second turn comes up, some drivers "brush" their horses, or let them go at top speed. Other drivers hold their horses back, or "rate" them, if the pace is too fast. Since many races are run at speeds of twenty-five to thirty miles per hour for the mile, horses often need to be held back to keep from tiring before the homestretch.

At the end of the first half mile, some drivers will try to move towards first place. Some drivers still hold back, waiting for the final moments. Coming

The starting gate speeds up to 35 mph before the gates swing out of the way to start the race.

up to the three-quarter-mile mark, all drivers and horses begin trying for the number one spot. It is at this time that a few horses tire and slip back, while others still have an extra burst of speed and move ahead. These horses scramble into the homestretch and fight for the lead spot. With so many good Standardbreds racing today, the battle down to the finish wire is always close and exciting.

Each year the top races for pacers are the Little Brown Jug Classic which is held in Delaware, Ohio; the William H. Cane Futurity held in Yonkers, New

Pictured is a race at the Hambletonian Classic for three-year-old trotters.

34

York; and the Messenger Stakes held in Westburg, Long Island, New York.

The top races for trotters are the Hambletonian held in East Rutherford, New Jersey; the Yonkers Futurity in New York; and the Kentucky Futurity held in Lexington.

TYPES OF RACES

There is a holiday air around the track when thousands of people come out to see the top

35

Standardbreds compete. Harness horses may race different kinds of races. They are: conditioned races, claiming races, stakes and futurities, early and late closing races, open, free-for-all races, and invitational races.

Only certain types of horses are run together in conditioned races. For instance, a conditioned race might be for "three-year-old trotting colts, winners of only two races at this meeting." The conditions of this race are spelled out for gait, age, sex, and number of races won.

We have already talked about claiming races in Chapter Three. Stakes are races in which a horse is entered a year before the race is run. In futurities, the horse is entered while it is still being carried by its mother.

In early closing races, horses are entered at least six weeks before the race. In late closing races, horses may be entered in the race only a few days before the race is to take place.

Open and free-for-all races are held for the fastest horses at any meeting. At an invitational race, the racing secretary at the track invites only the horses wanted for that race.

The complete rules and regulations of harness racing are to be found in the United States Trotting Association handbook. These rules govern the horses, breeders, owners, trainers, drivers, and race tracks.

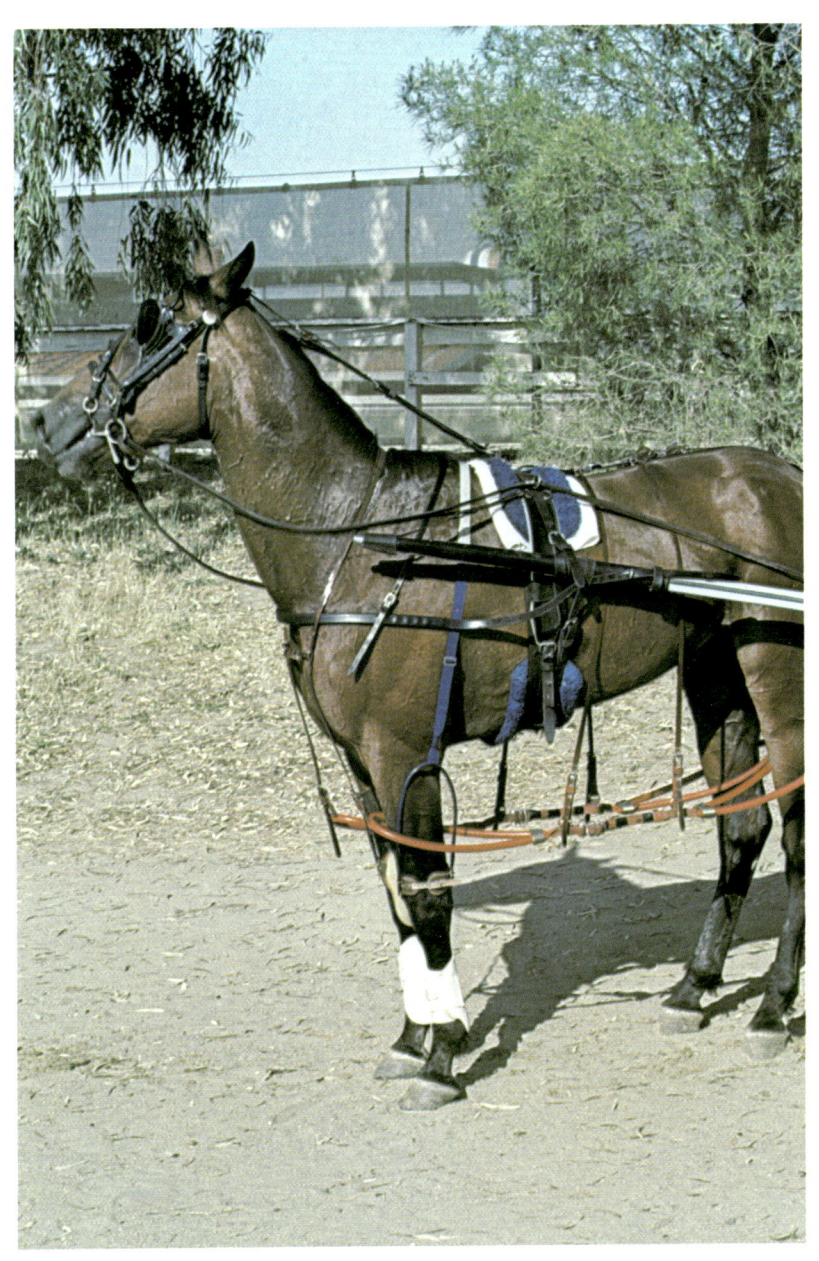

Shown above is a pacer and its tack.

The governing bodies in Canada are the Canadian Trotting Association and the Provincial Racing Commission.

A trotter (left) and a pacer (right).

⑤ THE CAST OF CHARACTERS

Harness racing is a partnership between horses and the people who own, breed, train, care for, and drive them. Let's look at the cast of characters who take care of these great horses.

38

OWNERS AND BREEDERS

An owner can be anyone. He or she can be the person who owns one harness horse and stables it in their backyard. The owner can be a farmer who owns a few harness horses and keeps them on the farm. It's just a hobby with owners like these and they race their horses only a few times a year at county fairs around the country.

The owner can also be a business man or woman who owns Standardbreds as their business. Although the owners may love horses, they are also in the horse business to make money.

Breeders are people who might be owners, but have another interest in horses as well. They breed, or mate, stallions to mares in order to raise the foals for sale. Breeding has become both a business and a science.

Before breeding a stallion to a mare, the breeder will study the "blood lines" of each horse. This means the breeder will study everything there is to know about a horse's ancestors.

The breeder must also study a horse's conformation — the way it looks. A breeder will carefully note the color of the grandparents' and parents' coats. Whether they have long legs or short, strong shoulders or weak ones, small or large heads, and short or long necks is also noted. A foal will get some of these same traits from its ancestors.

Racing history tells us that when a horse often wins, it has fast horses in its background. Therefore, when a racing champion becomes too old to race any more, it often moves to a breeding farm to become a parent to a future champion racer.

TRAINERS AND DRIVERS

Some people say the trainer is the most important person in the harness horse's life. The trainer takes

Drivers urge their horses on as they approach the finish line.

over the life of a yearling on the day it begins to learn about harness racing. The trainer and a horse will work together everyday of its racing life until the horse retires. The trainer will direct the exercise of a horse, control the animal's feed, keep the horse happy and content, and teach it to become a winner.

Owners of Standardbreds may go from track to track to find a skilled trainer. They may write to the Harness Horsemen's Association for names of trainers. The right trainer can make a horse into a champion.

More than twelve thousand men and women are

now driving harness horses in the United States. Many more drive in Canada and Europe. Some of them are amateurs. For most of the drivers, their only payment is the joy of driving. However, many of them are professionals who make their living at it. All of them are in it because they love the sport and the horses.

Most of the drivers have been around horses all their lives just as the trainers have. In fact, many drivers are also trainers.

In addition to knowing horses and loving them, drivers must also have "light hands." Hands are an important tool used to "talk" to a horse during training and during a race. The driver must tell the horse through control of the reins when to move, when to turn, when to slow down, and when to speed up.

Harness race drivers wear their own "colors" during a race. These jackets and helmets are made with the drivers' own choice of design and color.

SPECIAL HELP

A veterinarian is someone who has studied long years in school to be an animal doctor. The vet will have a degree in veterinary medicine.

If a mare has trouble foaling, a vet may be called in to help. If a newborn is weak, the vet will know how to help the foal gain weight and strength. Later, the

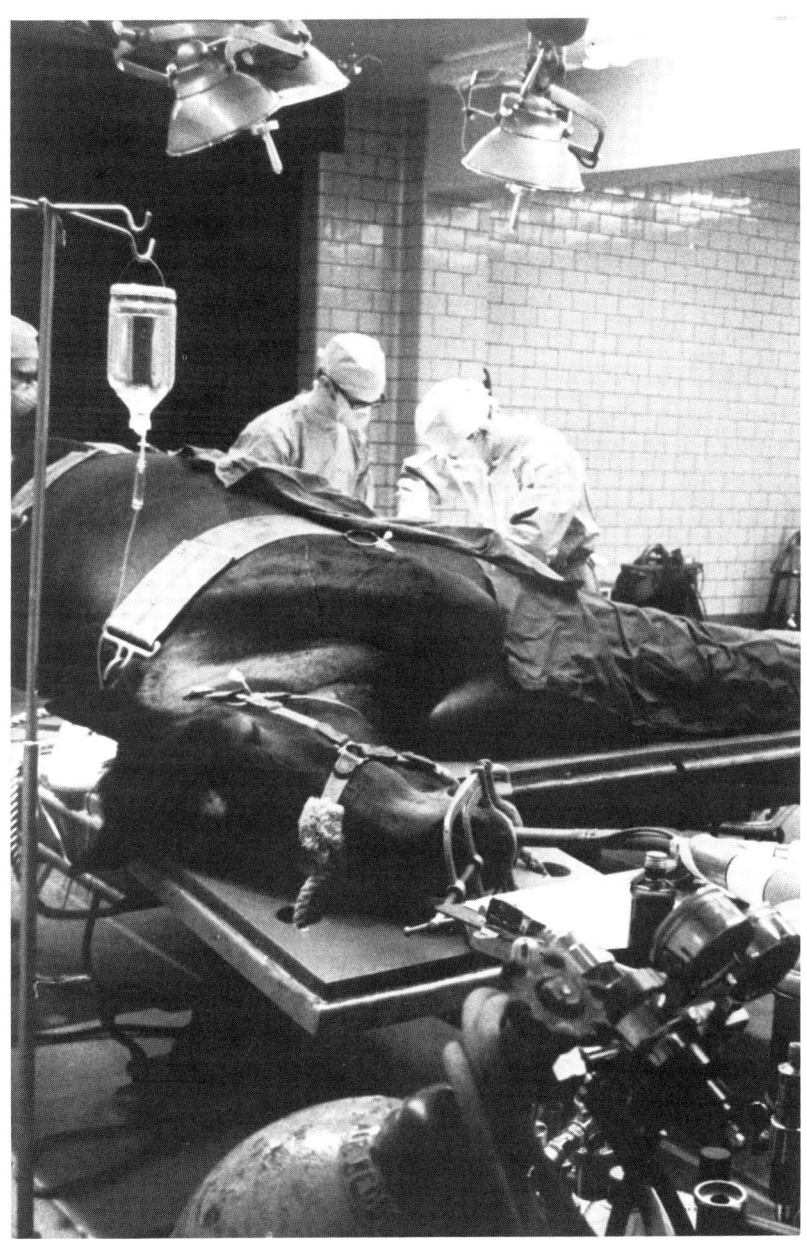

This horse is having surgery to repair an injured leg.

vet will give the foal its shots to keep it from catching different diseases.

Should a horse become ill or lame, the vet may have to bandage its legs, or give medicines to help the horse return to health.

A blacksmith, also called a farrier, is another important person to the harness racing horse. Most harness horses wear out a set of shoes every month. If the horse has a special gait it must also have special shoes. Sometimes the trainer may try different shoes on a horse to improve its speed. If a horse has problems with its legs or hoofs, the blacksmith and veterinarian will work closely together to overcome them.

⑥ AFTER RACING DAYS ARE OVER

Champion stallions and mares will often retire to breeding farms when they become too old to race. They will enjoy life in rolling green pastures and pass their champion genes on to their foals. Once in awhile, these horses will make "guest" appearances at special racing events. These events help raise money for worthwhile causes.

Often times an outstanding champion will be elected to the Hall of Fame of the Trotter where it will always be remembered. Awards, trophies, statues, and pictures in the Hall of Fame keep the memories of harness racing champions alive. The Hall of Fame is located in a beautiful building in Goshen, New York, not far from the place where the great Messenger once grazed. To harness racing fans everywhere, it seems just the right place for the Hall of Fame to be.

The Hall of Fame of the Trotter.

GLOSSARY

BIT - A metal bar that is part of the bridle which fits into a horse's mouth.

BRIDLE - The headgear used to control a horse. The main parts are the reins and bit.

BRUSH - A burst of speed in a race or during training.

CHECKREIN - A line to keep a horse's head held high.

COLT - A young male horse.

CONFORMATION - The way a horse looks; it's shape.

COOLING OUT - Walking a horse after a race or training until its heartbeat returns to normal.

FARRIER - A blacksmith who places metal shoes on a horse's hoofs.

FILLY - A young female horse.

FOAL - A newborn horse, male or female.

GAIT - The way in which a horse walks or moves.

GIRTH - A strap that fits under a horse's stomach.

HALTER - A piece of equipment that fits around a horse's head and is used for leading or tying.

HOBBLES - Gear worn by a pacer to keep him in pacing gait.

HOT HORSE - One who has just finished a race or training period and needs to be cooled out.

JOG CART - A sulky that is heavier and longer than a regular cart. It is used for training and warm-ups.

MARE - A female horse.

PADDOCK - The area at the track where horses are kept before a race.

RATE A HORSE - To hold a horse back and keep him from running too fast in a race.

SIRE - A father of horses.

STALLION - A male horse.

STANDARDBRED - An American breed of horse used for harness racing.

STARTER - The official at a race who decides when a race starts.

SULKY - A light racing cart with bicycle-type wheels used in harness racing.

TACK - Racing and stable equipment.

WEANLING - A foal which has been taken from its mother, when it is about four or five months old.

YEARLING - An age given to every Standardbred on the first of January after its birth. Since most horses are born in the spring, they usually become yearlings at about seven to ten months of age.

THE HORSES
PASTURE TO PADDOCK

READ & ENJOY THE ENTIRE SERIES:

RUFFIAN
THE PONIES
THOROUGHBREDS
HUNTERS & JUMPERS
PLEASURE HORSES
HARNESS RACING
RODEO HORSES
DRAFT HORSES

CRESTWOOD HOUSE